P9-CBE-437

spot

SPORTS

VOLLEYBALL

by Mari Schuh

AMICUS | AMICUS INK

coach

baseline

Look for these words and pictures as you read.

net

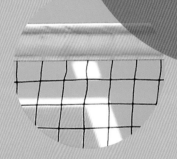

knee pad

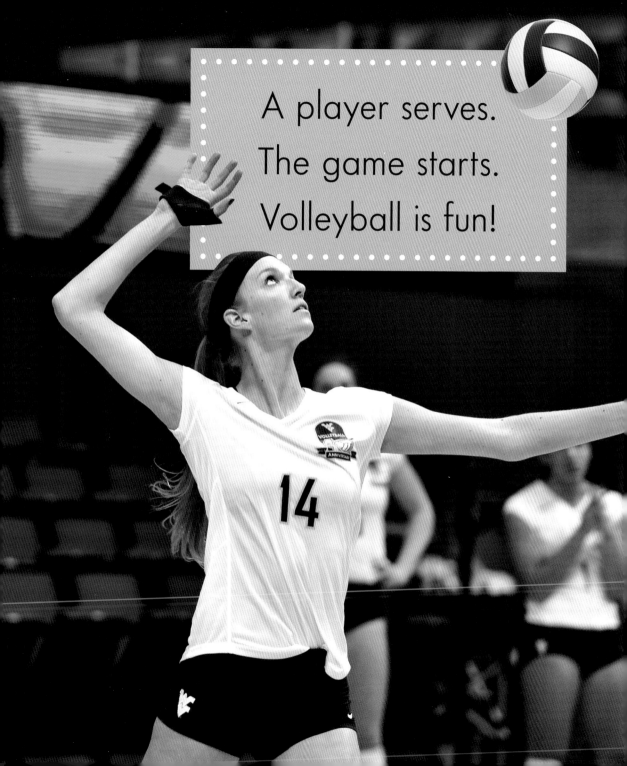

A player serves.
The game starts.
Volleyball is fun!

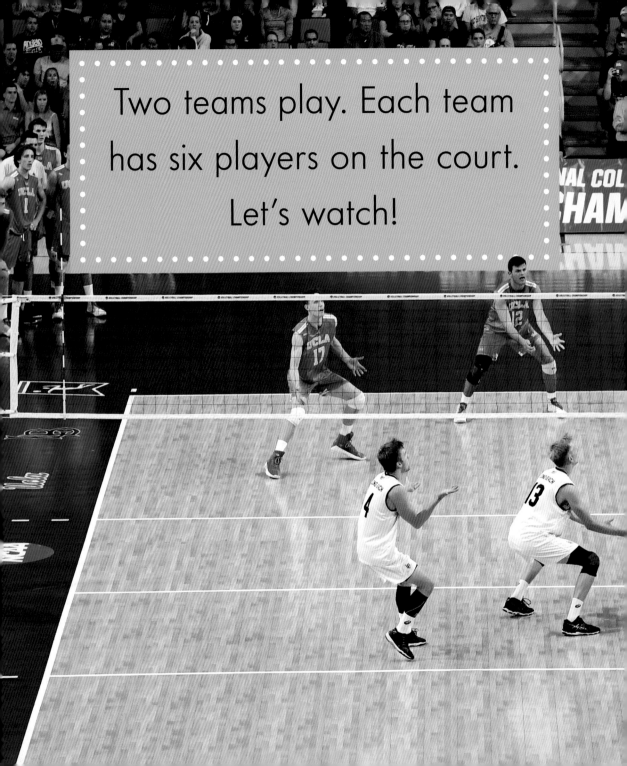

Two teams play. Each team has six players on the court. Let's watch!

Do you see the coach?
She leads her team. Let's win!

coach

Do you see the baseline?
A player serves there.
Way to go!

baseline

Do you see the net?
A player spikes the ball.
It goes over the net.
Bam! One point!

net

Do you see the knee pads?
Pads keep his knees safe.
He can slide to get the ball.

knee pad

The players jump. They block the ball. Good job!

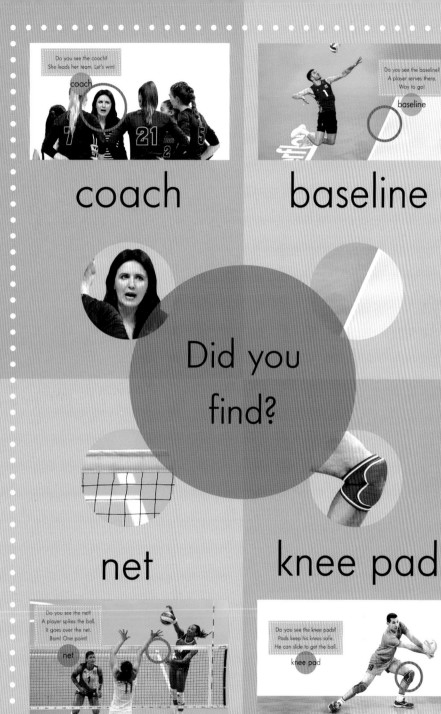

Do you see the coach?
She leads her team. Let's win!

coach

coach

Do you see the baseline?
A player serves there.
Way to go!

baseline

baseline

Did you find?

Do you see the net?
A player spikes the ball.
It goes over the net.
Bam! One point!

net

net

Do you see the knee pads?
Pads keep his knees safe.
He can slide to get the ball.

knee pad

knee pad

Spot is published by Amicus and Amicus Ink
P.O. Box 1329, Mankato, MN 56002
www.amicuspublishing.us

Library of Congress Cataloging-in-Publication Data
Names: Schuh, Mari C., 1975- author.
Title: Volleyball / by Mari Schuh.
Description: Mankato, Minnesota : Amicus, [2020] |
Series: Spot. Sports | Audience: K to Grade 3.
Identifiers: LCCN 2018034291 (print) | LCCN 2018036184
 (ebook) | ISBN 9781681517377 (pdf) | ISBN 9781681516554
 (library binding) | ISBN 9781681524412 (pbk.)
Subjects: LCSH: Volleyball--Juvenile literature. | Picture
 puzzles--Juvenile literature.
Classification: LCC GV1015.34 (ebook) | LCC GV1015.34 .S38
 2020 (print) | DDC 796.325--dc23
LC record available at https://lccn.loc.gov/2018034291

Printed in China

HC 10 9 8 7 6 5 4 3 2 1
PB 10 9 8 7 6 5 4 3 2 1

For Tabitha —MS

Wendy Dieker, editor
Deb Miner, series designer
Aubrey Harper, book designer
Holly Young, photo researcher

Photos by iStock/skodonnell
cover, 16; Shutterstock/fotoinfot
cover, 16; Shutterstock/Eugene
Onischenko 1; Shutterstock/
Aspen Photo 3; Getty/John W.
McDonough 4–5; Getty/Icon
Sportswire 6–7; AP/Robin Alam/
Icon Sportswire 8-9; Getty/Buda
Mendes 10-11; Alamy/Radek
Petrasek/CTK 12–13; Shutterstock/
CP DC Press 14-15

VOLLEYBALL